MW00462577

© 2004 Bobcat Press

UK Edition
Bobcat Press
242 Clarendon Street, Manchester M15 5AB
info@bobcatpress.com
www.bobcatpress.com

ISBN 0 9529517 2X

North American Edition
Quick American
Oakland, CA 94606
www.quickamerican.com

ISBN: 0-932551-65-3

First edition.
Printed in China.

Text, design and illustration by Bobcat
Proof reading by Natalie Holland

This book is dedicated to Kathryn Pemberton for better reasons than could be described here.

Dear Reader,

what with spliff smoking more entrenched in mainstream culture than fish and chips and reality TV, you'd be forgiven for thinking that cannabis was now legal, or at least not as illegal as it used to be....

Anyway, we are legally obliged to point out that the posession, supply or cultivation of cannabis is still very much against the law. Please note: this does still apply to terminally ill patients dependant on cannabis for pain relief, so don't start thinking YOU'RE special or anything.

The information in this book is published purely for the satisfaction of foolish and idle curiosity and not to promote a dangerous rock'n'roll lifestyle of earthly pleasure (which you'll only regret later on). Whilst the laws against cannabis remain, this book is not intended to encourage you to break them.

so be nice and good
Bobcat

CONTENTS

LET'S GO! >

CONGRATULATIONS!

By picking up this book, you just took your first step on the long, winding path to becoming a true joint-rolling master. It's a journey you won't regret, yet the way of the joint-rolling über ninja is not always an easy one. The spectre of confusion may even pluck at your sleeve and ask:

"Wasn't there something more important you should have been doing?"

Ignore such petty distractions! Focus on the rewards. All you need is patience, skill and a big heap of fine herb. Remember, perfection takes time: career breaks, academic holidays, prison spells, days spent trapped in wells – all are ideal opportunities to hone your craft and develop some fly skills.

Eyes down, fingers limber…get rollin'!

FUNDAMENTALS

The Mix

*Y*our joint might look like the pinnacle achievement of a dextrous craftsman, but if it tastes like a burning tractor tyre or lacks the required oomph, then your creation is a failure. Put simply, what goes into your joint determines how good it's going to be.

A GOOD MIX IS EVERYTHING

Even if it resembles something a cow spat out, a joint that tastes good and 'hits the spot' is always a success. For this you need good ingredients. Luckily, thanks to indoor gardening, and an increasingly savvy customer base, the dark ages of Moroccan 'soap bar' seem to be almost behind us and good bud—if not good hash—can be found almost everywhere.

Around the world at cannabis cups, conventions and private parties, thousands of plant strains and brands of fine bud and hashish are being judged not just on the nature of the high but also their aroma, flavour, burning qualities and appearance.

In the past few years, cannabis conoisseurs have reached equally dizzying new heights of both pseudery and sophistication.

Back in the shadow of prohibition, the finer points of cannabis selection can seem pointless to many smokers when the menu is limited to what 'Tall Dave' managed to get hold of that week. Still, knowing how to separate the good shit from the bad shit can help you to bargain with your dealer, blag your way in connoisseur circles and look cool at parties. Read on.

ROLLING WITH BUD

Nowadays, thanks to indoor growing techniques, a prime plump bud of legendary quality can be grown pretty much anywhere on the planet. We no longer have to hop continents in search of a good smoke – in fact, the better bud in your mix bowl is far more likely to have sprouted in Halifax or Keighley than in the Hindu Kush.

There are three keys to good bud. The first and most important is the **genetic makeup** of the donor plant. The inherent qualities of each cannabis strain have the most influence on the high. There are distinct and noticeable differences between strains —both in terms of the strength and the characteristics of the high. The second key is the **growing method**. Perfect conditions and good gardening are needed for a plant to achieve its full potential. The final key to truly great bud is in the careful **drying, curing and preparation**

of the finished product – tasks too often neglected in the chase for profit. All three factors have a crucial effect on the quality of cannabis, so how do you pick the good shit from the bad shit?

TEST 1: GIVE IT A SNIFF

For most people, smoking weed is about getting high, not droning on about the olfactory subtleties of a bit of plant matter, but pretensions aside, your nose can tell you a lot about the quality of cannabis.

Nicely cured bud purrs out a wide spectrum of different and distinct aromas and no two varieties are the same. The overall effect should be strong but complex and it should be fragrant straight from the bag—if you need to shake or pinch cannabis to get a good whiff then something is not right. If the bud smells sharply of chlorophyl (like a freshly mown wet

lawn) then the curing process has been bungled or omitted. Check musty-smelling bud for any mould or decay. Don't risk a lung infection: weed that has gone 'off' should be binned and your dealer sacked.

TEST 2: TAKE A LOOK

Hold the bud up to the light and examine it closely. Hopefully, what you are looking at are thousands of glistening dots, spread over the surface of the bud. These tiny sparklers are resin glands swollen with THC and bursting with promise. The more of them the better, as these are what will get you high.

Buds are delicate. With rough handling the fragile resin glands fall away and potency is depleted. A pile of dust and fragments at the bottom of the bag is a sign of ill treatment. Intact buds look fluffy but feel solid, they should retain the natural shape they held whilst growing on the plant. Leaf roughens the smoke and bud properly presented for sale should have had its leaves trimmed as closely as possible

TEST 3: ROLL IT UP

Roll the bud pure for an accurate test, leave your tobacco or mixer for later. Perfectly cured bud crumbles softly and easily between the fingers, releasing a wealth of heady aromas and tacky resins. Stems should flex a little but eventually snap when bent. Bendy stems and a 'squidgy' feel mean too much moisture. Ask for a 'wet' discount as your deal could shrink by 20% overnight as it dries.

TEST 4: SPARK IT UP

A toke on an unlit joint can give a good idea of quality through flavour and aroma but the definitive trial is by fire. Spark the joint (use a gas lighter) and smoke it up. The bud should burn smoothly all the way down to the roach and leave nothing but soft, pure ash.

Joints made from some weed will start great and then collapse into a tarry, acrid mess, others will pop, fizzle and burp as they burn. These are bad signs and could indicate residues of toxic chemical fertilisers or

pesticide which a competent grower would have been leached out of the plant before harvesting.

Pure cannabis joints have a tendency to make people cough. Whilst this is a normal (some even claim beneficial) part of the experience, when rolled and toked with care, good bud should smoke smooth and taste pleasant the whole way down the joint. Real throat-biting weed is best relegated to the vapouriser and water pipe—better yet, use it to cook with.

TEST 5: HOW DO YOU FEEL?

The judging of the high itself is entirely down to personal taste—whatever the experts or psueds tell you. Some enjoy a heavy, soporific down—others relish a speedy hallucinogenic high; some want a pleasant glow to their evening—others want to establish contact with their ancestors. Whatever flies your kite. The array of unique experiences to be had from different types of bud is worth exploring and there are a plethora of varieties out there to suit every taste and occasion.

STORING BUD

Once you've made your choice, you need to take care of your purchase. Remember: buds are delicate flowers and need to be treated with care to be enjoyed at their best. Don't crush, shake or otherwise mishandle your stash.Properly cured bud is best stored in a sealed container, away from heat, moisture and light. A plastic tub with a lid is as good as anything else.Bud that is still damp should be kept in a paper bag in a warmish room until it reaches the right state Don't seal damp weed in plastic, it will fester and spoil. Dry, aging weed that has withered into a hot, harsh smoke can be rescued with an old smoker's trick. Store it in a plastic bag with a little piece of lemon peel. In less than a day it should have returned, at least some of the way, to it's former glory.

COMPACTED BUD AND IMPORTS

Imported bud is often crushed and pressed into blocks to ease smuggling, storage and transport.

Quality is variable, with handfuls of seed and stem packed in there with the bud, but don't be too quick to write off scrappy-looking 'bush'. Whilst it may not meet some of the tests on the previous pages, the original bud was often of exceptional quality and the effects might just be to your liking...

PREPARING BUD FOR ROLLING

Bud should be broken into smallish fragments of similar size—think light, fluffy, crumbly and even. The mix needs to allow air to pass through the joint, so try not to pinch or compress the fragments. A pair of sharp scissors makes things much easier, and a bud grinder (available at a headshop near you) will break a delicate bud into a perfect mix in seconds, without wastage. Of all the paraphenalia targeted at joint rollers, a grinder is most worth a dip in your pocket.

For a smooth smoke, take some care to remove ALL the stalks, leaves and any other debris you might find in the mix. Anything that feels woody should certainly be ejected. If you are using seeded weed (it still exists) take particular care to get all seeds and fragments of seeds out of the mix Cannabis seeds will not get you stoned and they are harmful and foul-tasting when smoked. Chuck them in the garden.

When blending bud with tobacco (or some other mixer), it is important to get all the ingredients to a similar consistency for a smooth and even burn. Use a mix bowl or the palm of your hand and blend with your fingers. Use a light touch but be thorough.

ROLLING WITH HASHISH

*H*ashish—at least hashish in its purest form—is made by rubbing or shaking the resin glands from the female cannabis plant and then hand-working or machine pressing them into a solid piece. There is something very exotic about the idea of Buddhist monks, high in the Himalayan foothills, harvesting sacred resins from ancient strains of powerful Indica cannabis and hand working them into precious opiated balls of stupefyingly rich hashish. Unfortunately, the reality, at least for the most part, is more prosaic. The solids industry has been dominated for decades by a mountain of cheap, fraudulent Moroccan offerings which probably represent some of the worst hash that has ever existed. The massive UK market has long been viewed as the perfect dumping ground for this appalling soap bar or melange, which typically consists of the sweepings from the factory floor combined with a motley array of other ingredients that have never seen a cannabis plant. THC contents of less than 0.4% (or even zero) are not unusual. Thankfully the future of hash is looking brighter.

As modern-day Dutch pioneers, like Mila Jansen, reinvent the ancient art of hash-making with astonishing results, and the odd lump of Parvatti cream or genuine Moroccan Pollen still make it past the profiteers, good hashish is maybe a little less rare than it once was. Follow the following tests to know if you've strayed across some of the good stuff .

TEST 1: GIVE IT A SNIFF

Without wanting to insult anyone's intelligence cannabis should smell like cannabis. If it doesn't, it is of low quality, very old or it is simply something else. The aroma should be fresh and spicy, not stale or musty.

TEST 2: DROP IT

Good hashish is solid, dense stuff. Dropped onto a hard surface (glass or metal) you should hear a hard 'tick' rather than a dull 'thud'. Watch it doesn't roll under the sofa or land in your beer.

TEST 3: PLAY WITH IT!

Hashish that feels soft and 'squidgy' at room temperature may be adulterated with oil or fat and is best avoided. When cool, good hashish should feel firm and slightly tacky to the touch. Cutting with a sharp blade should leave a smooth, hard edge.

TEST 4: PLAY WITH IT!

After some vigorous warming in your hand, good hashish will be transformed: its aroma will increase and it will become very pliable. With a little heat, you should be able to mould pieces of top quality hashish into any shape you like and blend together separate pieces. If hash remains hard or brittle after being warmed, then the resin content is low.

TEST 5: GIVE IT A NIBBLE

A test for the brave as hashish has been known to contain the odd bit of camel dung and may well have passed through the hands of people who only see

soap when it's on TV. Good hashish tastes peppery, a little bitter, and does not dissolve easily in the mouth.

TEST 6: BURN IT

Hashish will catch and then burn in a similar way to an incense stick. If a piece lights immediately and burns readily, it could be adulterated with oils or candle wax. If it continually goes out, the hash probably contains little resin or has been sitting in a someones cellar for far too long. Good hash is reluctant to take a flame but it will burn with a steady ember once lit. White or bluish smoke is an excellent sign whereas black or dark brown smoke may mean adulterants. After burning, quality hash will leave nothing more than a soft, pale ash. Hash that leaves a dark, gritty residue should arouse suspicion.

   The best part of a burning test is to inhale the smoke and try out your new aquisition for real. As with any cannabis, judging a high is purely a matter of personal taste and preference, but genuine hash is naturally powerful stuff, a feeble high is a sign of impurities, harmful or not. An empty 'woozy' high that does not feel like cannabis can mean chemical additives, although if the hash passes all the other tests this is unlikely. For a credible test, it is best to smoke the hash pure (see the joint section for some pure smoking ideas).

HASH THAT FAILS THE TESTS

The melange, formula (fake resin) and soap bar widely sold as hash in the UK and other parts of Europe can be convincing to the eye, but they will fail some or all of these tests. Smokers should avoid this noxious stuff at all costs – even if they enjoy the milder 'high'. The chemicals (such as benzene) that are often mixed into bogus hash to mimic or bolster genuine effects, are potentially dangerous. No research has been carried out into the health consequences of smoking adulter-ated hash – a worrying thought when you consider the millions who smoke it on a daily basis.

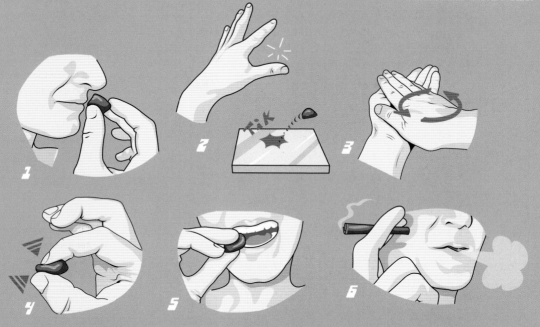

TiK

PREPARING HASH FOR ROLLING

The popular method of prepping hash for a joint is to heat the piece until it can be crumbled into small fragments and added to the mix. This is quick and easy but care is needed to avoid degrading the taste and high by applying too much heat, or (as many people do) by actually setting light to the stuff. When warming hash with a flame, remember to **toast not torch**.

Slower but less harmful, is to simply pick out fragments of hash using your thumbnail. By warming it in the hand, even hard hash can be made soft enough to pick at without the use of a damaging flame.

Soft hashish can be rolled into long thin 'sausages' and laid along the length of the joint. Some hash smokers swear by the 'sausage roll', claiming it guarrantees an even distribution for the whole joint as well as cutting down on hot rock disasters.

Harder hash can be 'shaved' into the mix as powder or paper-thin slivers with the aid of a razor blade. This is a great way to totally preserve the flavour and high of the hash whilst still creating an efficient and thorough blend that will smoke smoothly. It is by far the best way to make a hash-dense joint smoke evenly. If your hash is too soft to shave, ten minutes in a freezer will solve the problem.

RESIN POWDER

Rolling with resin powder (essentially, unpressed hash) is simplicity itself. The powder is simply sprinkled over the mix and blended in.

CANNABIS OIL

If you find yourself in posession of this rarity (genuine oils are scarcer than WMD) the standard method is to smear it onto a rolling paper or standard cigarette and then smoke them as normal. This is easy but actually quite wasteful. A better but messier method is to work the oil into the mix and roll it inside the joint.

COOK AND CRUMBLE

SAUSAGE ROLL

SHAVE AND POWDER

ROLLING WITH MIXERS

A mixer is anything other than cannabis that is rolled into the joint. Joint mixers have an enhancing role similar to the kind of mixers you find behind a bar: they prolong the experience and improve the flavour. Additionally, they may regulate and smooth the burn of the joint.

WHY USE A MIXER?

Padding out a joint with a mixer (usually tobacco) relaxes the smoking experience. Suddenly, no one is counting how many drags are taken or worrying that there won't be enough to go around. That indefinable 'druggy' tension that can marr the enjoyment of a pure joint is replaced with something altogether more civilised and sociable. People sit back and take time to share and savour a smoother tasting smoke.

TOBACCO

As the number one choice of mixer, tobacco has an association with cannabis that stretches back for centuries. Despite an ever expanding exile from 'respectable' society, it still bulks out the majority of joints rolled in Europe. The smoking of tobacco joints is especially entrenched in hashish-using cultures that already have a yen for the 'evil' weed. Hashish and tobacco (kif) are inseparable in Moroccan culture, for instance. Similarly, in Britain, France and Spain, (all incidentally countries awash with North African hashish) smoking cannabis almost invariably means smoking tobacco too. The two drugs undoubtedly compliment each other, but the persuading compulsion for nicotine makes a more convincing explanation for their union than any 'subtle frisson' of contrasting qualities.

There are also practical reasons for choosing tobacco as a mixer: commmercial tobacco is a quality assured smoking product; it is easily available everywhere; relatively affordable; and, for those hooked on the stuff, it saves rolling a joint and a cigarette.

NICOTINE-FREE MIXERS

Smoking tobacco in joints is a big mistake for a non-smoker. It's a common way to pick up (or return to) a 20-a-day habit. A habit which, (without wanting to re-tread well-journeyed ground), can take decades to shed, providing it doesn't kill or cripple first. Tobacco addiction, with the attendant risks of disease and slow death is, without much doubt, the number one health concern for cannabis users.

For those who want to avoid tobacco but would prefer not to smoke pure cannabis, nicotine-free smoking mixtures are the only option. A huge variety of herbal concoctions are widely available from head shops, health food outlets and good tobacconists.

The flavours range from pleasant to truly repellant, with the majority stinking out the tents in the latter camp. Finding a brand you actually like amongst the dross is a goal worth experimenting for.

DO I NEED A MIXER...?

Most connoisseurs claim that pure is the only way to go. Well-cured bud does not need to be mixed with anything at all. Broken and rolled correctly, pure bud will smoke smoothly and easily the whole way down the joint—it tastes good too. On the other hand, it is difficult, (although not impossible, see the Joints section) to roll a pure hashish spliff. Arguably, the best mixer for hashish is tobacco, but If you want to stay nicotine-free and still smoke hashish joints then you can use a herbal smoking mixture or, better still, mix the hash in with bud for a pure cannabis blend.

Papers

As the mighty redwoods were to the cabin building pioneers of the western frontier and the Scandinavian pines were to the people of Ikea, so cigarette papers are to the joint-roller. They are the materials of our craft and, as such, they are worth a closer lick…er…look.

IT GROWS ON TREES

According to tobacco lore, the first cigarette papers were invented in 19th century America by a nicotine-crazed bum looking for a means to smoke cigar butts discarded by passing rich folk. The pioneering skin used by this unsung hero was probably a piece of newsprint, or wrapping paper. Things have changed since these humble beginings (although the social status of cigarette smokers seems to be returning to it's roots). 150 years of unfettered economic progress and rampant

tree felling later…and now we can buy our rolling papers in blueberry flavour and printed with the Stars and Stripes. There are more varieties around now than there have ever been. So, which is the best?

LIGHT

HEAVY

PAPER WEIGHT

The weight of the paper has a big effect on how the joint will smoke. The lighter the paper the more porous (or leaky) it is likely to be. By allowing more air into the joint (and more smoke to escape), lighter papers deliver a smoother toke than heavier papers. The lightest papers are almost transparent and can feel fragile in the hands of a beginner. But apart from the hopeless cack-hands, liable to rip anything thinner than their shirts, this shouldn't put anyone off. With paper less is always more, paper never got anyone stoned and it doesn't improve the smoke.

The thicker the paper the less porous it will be. This means more smoke being channelled into your lungs and a harder, (but rougher) hit. Heavy or medium weight papers are useful when rolling very large joints that need the extra durability; and when smoking mixes that need an especially controlled burn – like overly dry bud, and or strong/pure hashish joints. In most other situations a lightweight paper will give a far better smoke. It's worth noting that where a paper overlaps it is twice as thick.

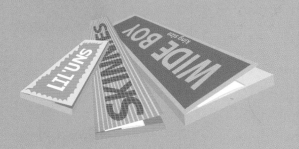

PAPER SIZE AND LENGTH

Wide papers are easy to roll with but are usually excessive for all but the fattest joints. Wide heavy papers that overlap (forming a doubl e or triple layer) are partculary hard on the throat. Remember: less is best. Calculate how much paper you will need and tear away any excess.

A wide paper offers great flexibility – you can always choose to tear it down to size. Narrow papers are fine if you only like to smoke long, thin, straight joints. Otherwise they are a pain in the arse.

Larger papers mean less difficult joins and a quicker roll. They do cost more though, and if discovered by some disapproving authority (like your mom) they leave little doubt as to their purpose. Little papers are less suspicious and they are cheap. More importantly-somehow it is more impressive when you make a big spliff out of them. Most of the joints in this book were made from standard small papers. If you want to boost the dimensions of any of the designs, just use a larger paper.

CUT CORNERS

Awww… Your first rolling paper. Brands with cut-away corners are marginally easier to roll and help beginners (or bewildered drunks) find the gummed edge. Handy in the dark, but much more suited to rolling cigarettes.

CONTINUOUS ROLL

A sort of minature toilet roll of cigarette paper that can be torn to the precise and desired length. Great idea, but check for quality.

PRINTED PAPERS

Camoflage, leopard skin and pearls of pseudo hippy nonsense can all be found printed onto rolling papers. And who are we to dictate taste? Most manafacturers use non-toxic soya inks but the fact that more chemicals are being thrown onto the bonfire is hard to escape. There is however, something satisfying about burning a national flag every now and again…

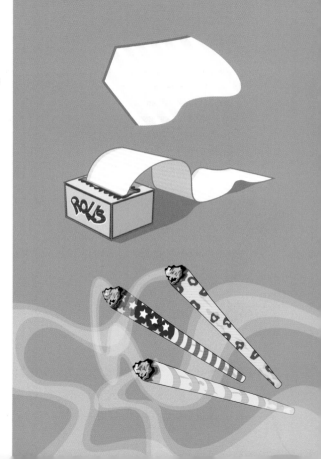

28

GUM STRIPPING

Gum stripping is an essential technique for advanced joint rollers. It involves tearing away the sticky part of the rolling paper and using it in your rolling. A gum-strip, once torn from its paper parent, becomes a piece of multi-purpose, joint-rolling construction tape. Perfect material for sealing leaking holes, joining joints to other joints and other exciting stuff. Kingsize papers with longer, wider gum strips are worth seeking out.

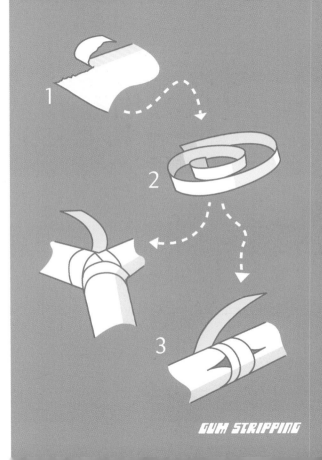

BLUNT WRAPS

People have been smoking herbs, wrapped in tobacco leaf, for thousands of years. Even the ancient Mayans enjoyed a blunt or two, so the latter-day trend of cannibalising cigars to make strong bud-packed blunts could be seen as the restoration of a rich cultural tradition. Links with US hip hop culture and an urban cool identity has earned the blunt a certain cachet, but there are other sirens beckoning smokers onto the welcoming rocks of Blunt Island. A cigar wrapper is less porous than a rolling paper and channels the smoke more directly into the lungs of the blunter. This makes for a harder kick, but the appeal of the blunt extends beyond mere grunt.

The synagesic effects of tobacco and cannabis are well known: the two herbs arguably improve and compliment each other's high and flavour. What is more, as you smoke a well rolled blunt, the slow-burning cigar wrapper mellows and restrains the hotter and quicker pace of the burning bud. All this, combined with the capacious and sturdy qualities of a cigar wrapper, make puffing on a blunt one of the better ways to consume a big heap of choice bud and look damn fly at the same time.

BLUNT WRAPS

Vacuum packed blunt wraps are readily available in a variety of styles and flavours. They can't be beaten for ease or convenience and are cheaper than most cigars, but the quality can be variable. Some brands are similar to the type of wrapper you might find around an economy cigar—not cured natural leaf but a processed paper made using tobacco. Nothing wrong in that, you might say, but if you're hankering after a premium smoke for a special occasion you might have to use a cigar.

WHICH CIGAR?

Picking a cigar to butcher for your blunt is down to personal taste. Phillies and White Owls are the traditional brand of choice for blunt rolling but this has more to do with fashion and price than quality or suitability. Natural leaf wrappers are considered a much smoother, tastier smoke than the cheaper tobacco paper hybrids, although they can be harder to roll and stick. Now, cigar purists may consider this a sacrilege…but if you're holding dope worthy of the treatment, why not tear into a really fine Cuban or Honduran stogie? Roll it up with some prize-winning bud, mixed in with a little Nepalese sticky to temper the burn, sit back and enjoy the best of both worlds.

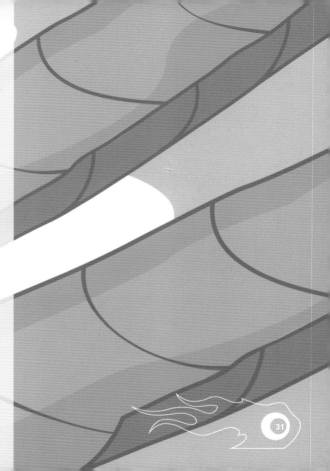

Rolling

Most people reading this book will be well practised in the art of rolling a decent spliff. If that includes you then turn some pages and head straight to the good stuff. On the other hand, if you are all flailing thumb, jabbing finger and wild slobbering tongue then read on, perhaps some basics will help.

PLACE THE MIX

If you are new to rolling, start with a single small paper. Avoid the very thin papers which can be difficult in the hands of a first timer. A nice durable skin like a Rizla green or red is perfect. Lay it down on a flat surface in front of you, with the gum strip facing upwards and on the far edge.

Blend the mix thoroughly. Take some time to ensure the mix is of a smooth and even consistency before placing it onto the paper.

Spread the mix evenly along the paper's length in a straight cylindrical shape, leaving a little gap at each end to allow for expansion.* The neater and tidier things are now, the easier the whole rolling process will be, and the better the end result. Spend a few seconds carefully arranging and shaping that mix along the paper.

*Adding a roach, which is often done at this stage, is probably best left for your second or third successful roll. See **Roaches** for techniques.

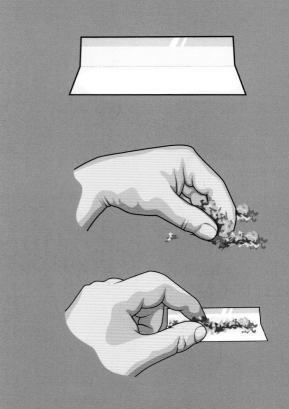

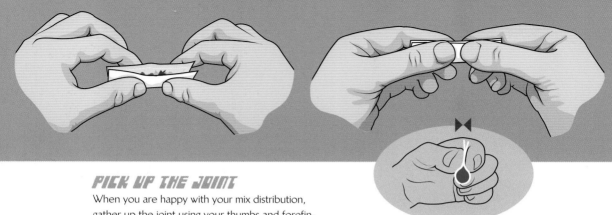

PICK UP THE JOINT

When you are happy with your mix distribution, gather up the joint using your thumbs and forefingers as shown. Gently but firmly, pinch the paper together, in the centre of the joint just above the mix—trapping it in the fold of the paper. The edges of the paper should be level.

Let the joint rest on your second fingers. Use your second fingers as steadying support whenever needed as you roll the joint.

ROLL THE JOINT

Now, for the rolling. Roll the mix up and then down, inside the paper. Let your thumbs do most of the work—like soft rolling pins against your forefingers. Your thumbs and forefingers should always be just above the mix, tightening the paper trap and

34

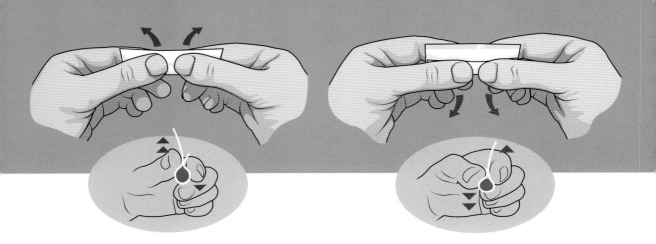

firming and compacting the mix. Start in the centre for your first roll and then move out along the joint as the mix firms and compacts. Roll until you can feel an even consistency across the length of the mix. Part of the trick is to know when to stop: too much and the joint will be tight and hard to draw

from—too little and you'll have a sorry flap-sack belching cinders in your lap. For a small joint, just two or three rolls should be enough.

With your final roll, take the mix down the paper until the ungummed edge is flush with the top of the mix. Now you're ready for the tuck'n'wrap.

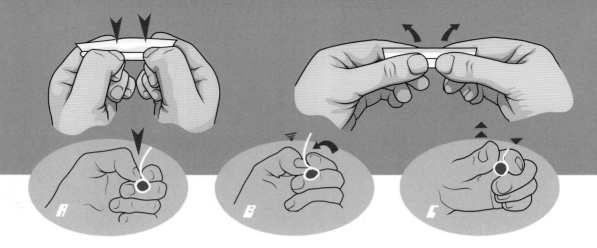

TUCK'N'TRAP

Tuck the ungummed edge over the mix and firmly down the other side as shown (*A*). A thumbnail is an advantage but not necessary. Work your way along the joint tucking that edge down with your thumb and trapping it with your forefingers (*B*).

Roll the mix all the way up the paper (*C*), leaving just the gum strip exposed. All that remains is to lick the gum (no slobbering now) and seal your first doobie! As a finishing flourish, twist the ends to prevent any leakage and celebrate in style by smoking your creation.

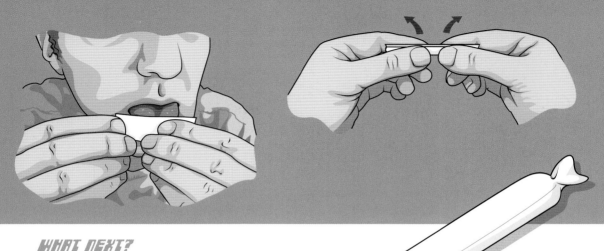

WHAT NEXT?

So, congratulations, you just rolled your first basic joint! Fancy it ain't, but now that you've nailed the basic technique, you can progress to rolling with a roach and making that perfect cone...

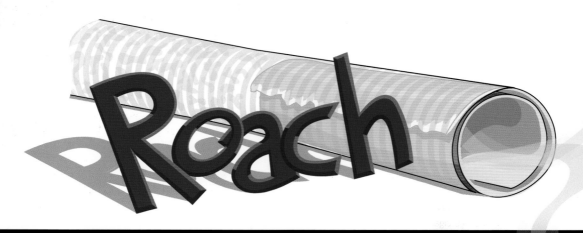

Roach

No joint is complete without a good roach. A cardboard tip allows free-flowing smoke, stops the joint from dissolving in your mouth; and protects your lips from smouldering herb as you chase that last elusive toke.

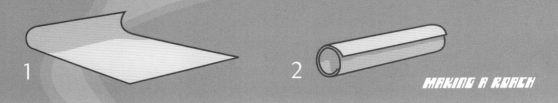

THE STANDARD ROACH

Shape and size are down to personal taste. A big bore roach can make the smoke hot and rough whereas a tight one can clog and make work for the smoker. Somewhere in the middle is probably best. An inch-long (2.5cm) roach is generally considered sufficient for most joints—a longer roach can mean a cooler smoke, but it leaves less room for the mix.

In terms of grade and weight, the card normally used to package cigarette papers is ideal. Try to use plain, unprinted and uncoated (i.e not shiny) card as there is a risk of poisonous fumes when some printing inks and varnishes are heated or burnt. To make your roach, simply tear or cut out a strip of card, approximately 1" x1.5" (2.5cm x 3.25cm) and roll it into a tube.

ROACH CLIP

An alternative to a card roach is to use a roach clip. This is typically a pair of tweezers or a croccodile clip which enable you to get the very last toke out of a pure weed, tip-less joint. Whilst a clip will protect your fingertips, your lips remain at risk of a blistering. Using a roach clip also has the unfortunate effect of making you look as if you're sucking vinegar through a tiny whistle. An unpleasant experience all round, and best avoided.

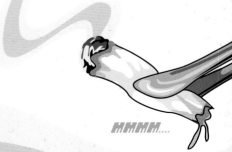

MMMM....

PLUG 'N' STUFF

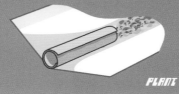
PLANT

CONICAL ROACH

PLUG 'N' STUFF [POST ROLL]

The most common approach. During the roll a gap is left at one end of the joint. After the joint has been rolled, a roach is made to fit the gap and inserted. Sometimes this goes well, sometimes it doesn't. More often than not, a certain amount of cajoling with a matchstick or similar 'pokey' is required to create a good fit. Great results are possible with the plug and stuff, but it demands skill and attention.

THE PLANT [PRE-ROLL]

Another method is to place the roach on the paper with the mix before rolling. The roach is treated as part of the mix and it is simply rolled in there along with everything else. Once perfected, the Plant is a far faster and much neater method.

THE CONICAL ROACH

An excellent variation on the simple tube roach. Tightly roll a 1" by 3" (2.5cm by 7cm) strip of thin card at a slight angle so that the end of the roach is conical. Roll your joint with the conical end of the roach facing outwards and let the card spring out a little to permit the smoke room to flow. A conical roach acts as a simple filter and makes a solid, durable tip.

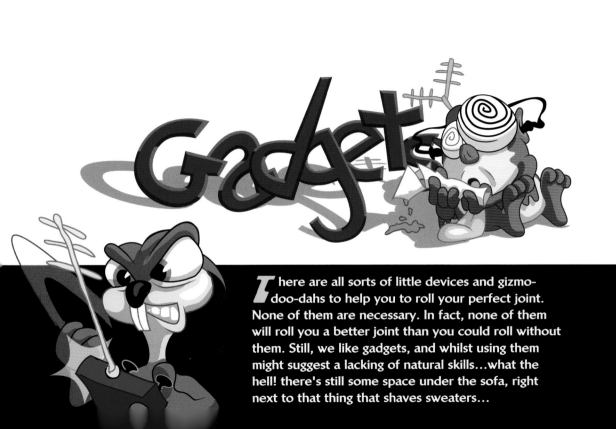

Gadget

There are all sorts of little devices and gizmo-doo-dahs to help you to roll your perfect joint. None of them are necessary. In fact, none of them will roll you a better joint than you could roll without them. Still, we like gadgets, and whilst using them might suggest a lacking of natural skills…what the hell! there's still some space under the sofa, right next to that thing that shaves sweaters…

BUD GRINDER

Something genuinely useful, everyone should own a bud grinder. A grinder is the easiest way to break up bud to an even consistency without any waste. Some have compartments to store your stash.

STANDARD ROLLING MACHINE

These aren't much cop. The long length models are sometimes useful but otherwise the standard rollers should be reserved for what they were designed to do: roll cigarettes.

ROLLING MAT

If your goal is a long, straight spliff, these work just as well as any rolling machine.

CONE ROLLER

A cunning design that aims to roll a perfect cone every time. The one we tried (Futurolla) worked pretty well, albeit after a short argument with the mechanism. Sadly, in the time it took us to find the thing (it was under the sofa) we could have rolled a fistful of hand-mades.

READY MADE CONES

Perfect machine-made cones with the roach already installed. How lazy can you get? The cones are placed in a plastic holder and then filled with mix. If you have arthritis or another condition that restricts full hand movement these are a solution.

METAL CONE

An interestingly simple design. Skins are rolled around the metal form to create an empty paper cone which is then filled with mix and plugged with a roach. The method gives good results, and can be used to roll a minimum paper joint. The downsides are a slow rolling speed and a fussy build..

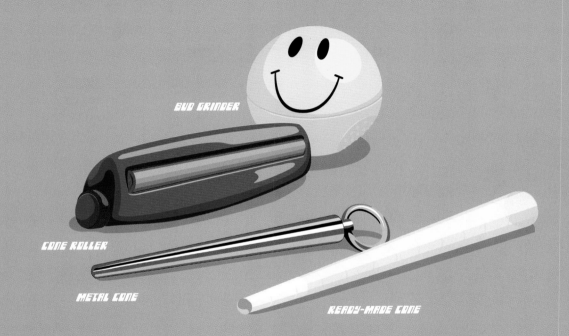

BUD GRINDER

CONE ROLLER

METAL CONE

READY-MADE CONE

THE JOINTS

PICK YOUR JOINT...

[IN ORDER OF DIFFICULTY]

DIFFICULTY

HIT POWER

ROLL SPEED

SMOKERBILITY

Hant a quick joint that's simple to roll and smokes smooth every time? A classic Easy Cone just can't be beat —after all, it's what you put in them that really counts. Here's three of the best quickies in town.

So, you've perfected your straight joint and now you're ready for more huh? Think you're something huh? Cool your jets bigshot, It's time to learn the way of the cone. Everyone likes a cone, but not everyone finds them easy to make…

The key is in the distribution of the mix. After you've laid out the papers, add the mix and then spend a little time forming it into a cone shape. Nothing complicated, you just need more at one end than at the other: a nice, evenly blended triangle. As you roll, aim for an even firmness and you'll feel a cone naturally forming itself in your fingertips. Go with it, let the cone come to you. Feeeeel the cone.

No? It's best to seal the papers from the roach to the tip. Wind the paper up, around the joint, tucking and tightening as you go. A cone is easier to roll with the roach already inside – seriously, trust us. Aim to match the dimensions of your roach with the estimated mix diameter after rolling – with a cone this should be pretty narrow. Perfectionists sometimes even make a cone-shaped roach to continue those tapering cone lines, let them.

Still no cone bliss? Tearing your papers into a more triangular shape can really help when building a cone – it encourages a good mix layout and means less annoying flap page at the narrow end when you come to roll. Once you've trimmed your paper, refold it along the centre length of the triangle to ease rolling..

1 Stick two papers together at a 45 degree angle as shown.

2 Add the mix and the roach. the layout of the papers makes the **Trembler** perfect for a cone-shaped creation.

3 When rolling the joint, stick down the first paper…

4 …before wetting the second paper and then wrapping it around to seal the smoking end of the joint.

*T*he fastest multi-skinned joint on the planet. Simple yet saucy, the **Knee Trembler** uses just two papers and can be rolled in seconds. The classic cone quickie.

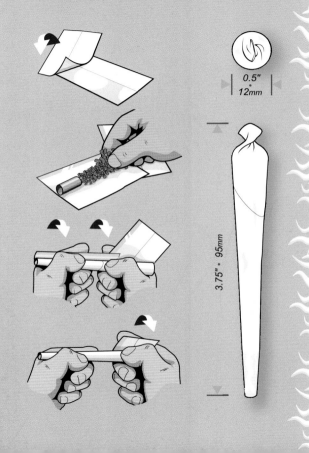

0.5"
12mm

3.75" • 95mm

EASY CONES

1 Stick two papers together with the gum strips forming a straight line. They should over-lap by about a fifth of their length.

2 Stick a third paper to the back of the first two, centering it in the middle of the number.

3,4 Add the mix and roach, the paper shape suits a slender cone or a straight joint. Roll as normal and enjoy!

Long-time classic to some, pointless fiddly mess to others. The **Saturday Night Special** suits a narrow cone but is heavy on paper for such a slender joint. A popular number nonetheless.

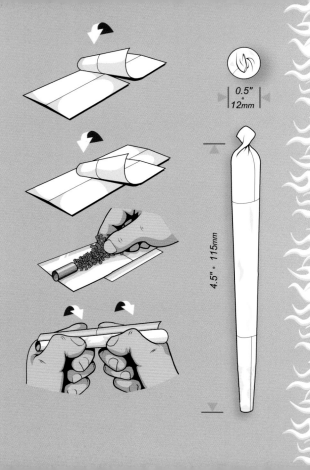

0.5"
12mm

4.5" • 115mm

1   Stick two papers together to form a square with a gum strip along one side.

2   Take a third paper and stick it, face down, to the end of the first two.

3   There is plenty of space for mix so it's best to trim away any excess paper (paper never got anyone stoned).

4   Roll the joint as normal, then twist the end to secure the third paper.

*F*or those that like 'em short, stubby and mean. Smoking a loaded **Magic Carpet** is like Joe Pesci hitting you about the head with a rolled-up rug. Well... something like that anyway.

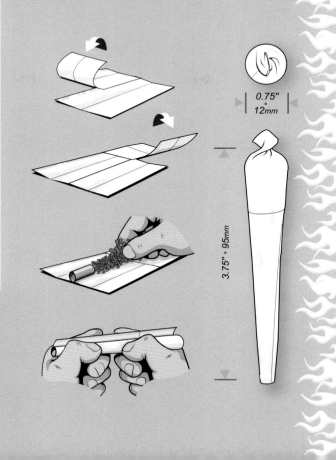

0.75" 12mm

3.75" • 95mm

EASY CONES

YODELLING

Don't fancy the look of that phlegm-oozing spitbag that the sweaty guy just passed you? Yodelling avoids contact between your mouth and the joint. Place the joint between your first and second fingers, cup your hands with thumbs and palms together and simply draw smoke from between your thumbs. Yodelling works great and is also excellent for cooling smoke, but you do run the risk of singeing a knuckle.

DIFFICULTY

HIT POWER

ROLL SPEED

SMOKERBILITY

Joint smoking often calls for discretion. If you're in need of a clandestine toke, roll yourself a Secret Agent, fold up your collar and remember to stay downwind.

1 Take a cigarette and remove the filter by squeezing at its base and rotating between finger and thumb. Eventually enough of the filter will show for you to get a hold and pull it out.

2 Replace the filter with a roach of the same size and shape.

3 Cut the cigarette in two, as cleanly as possible, about a quarter inch from the roach.

4 Stick two papers together to make a square with a gum strip along one side.

5 Make up enough mix to replace the tobacco that was cut away and add this to the papers. Form it into the shape of a cigarette.

6 Roll the joint with the 'filter' protruding from the end. You may need to secure the bogus filter with a gummed strip.

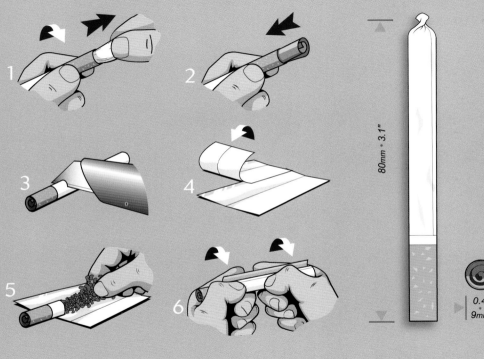

80mm • 3.1"

0.4" • 9mm

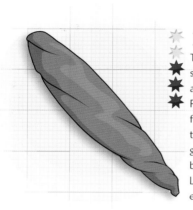

'AVA BANANA

Trapped in a tropical island paradise? Gagging for a spliff but your skins have amalgamated into a paper accordion, glued together by your own fair sweat? Fear not, nature is your help at hand! First you need to find a bananna tree (they're the ones with banannas on them), then you need to take a look around on the ground. Along with their many other fascinating uses, bananna leaves can also make pretty decent er...skins. Look for a leaf that is dry enough to burn but still pliable enough to roll with and give it a try.

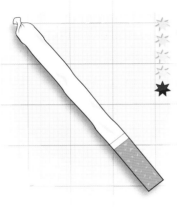

HOLIDAY CIGARETTE

No banana trees? This is a slightly duff version of the Secret Agent with the only advantage being that all you need is a cigarette and some weed. It takes ages, it's fiddly, it's boring and it's not so great when you've finished it but it's a joint, you're desperate —so stop whinging and get twiddling. Empty the cigarette using a rotating finger and thumb action but leave a tobacco 'plug' at the filter. Refill the tube with the mix pinch-by-pinch, using a pen or pencil as a ramrod between inserts. As a final touch, ease out the filter and replace it with a card roach.

fssssst

SIDE LICK

If one side of your joint burns faster than the other, the traditional method of recovery is to spot some spit on the faster burning side. Artfully dribbled, this should slow the burn and return some equilibrium to the situation.

Alternatively, a flame can be used to burn up the slow cooking side and keep the joint smoking how you'd like it. Keeping the consistency of the mix even and your rolling technique smooth should prevent any future lopsided disasters.

DIFFICULTY

HIT POWER

ROLL SPEED

SMOKERBILITY

JOKER

Size matters, so here's a number that seems to last forever. The Joker is a big, fat, juicy cone guaranteed to spread a grin from ear-to-ear without straining the finger muscles.

1 Stick two papers together, so that they form a straight line.

2 Take a third paper and fold it in two, leaving the gummed strip on the outside. Wet the glue and sandwich the folded paper firmly between the other two as shown.

3 Before the glue dries, pull the paper out. It will have left enough glue to stick the others together.

4 Stick a fourth paper to the lower, right-hand edge of the joint as shown.

5 Gum a fifth paper to the end of the joint as shown.

6 Create a more triangular shape by tearing the fourth paper diagonally in half. Refold the papers along the centre of this triangle to ease rolling.

7 To support the extra length use the whole of the forefingers when rolling. Get ready for some side-splitting entertainment.

60

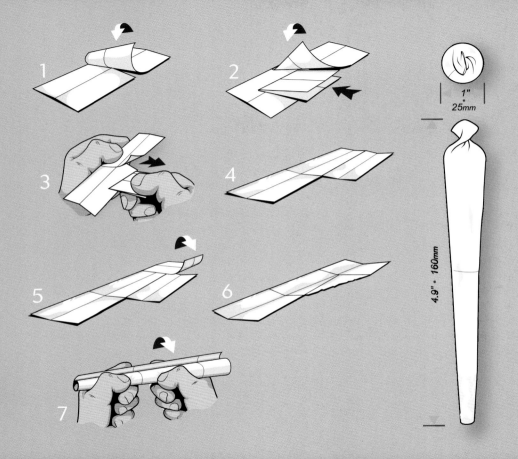

CEILING SCRAPER

Joker not long enough for you? Personal Rizla mountain nearing its sell by date? Napoleon complex? Then the Ceiling Scraper is the joint for you. There are two common methods for rolling a super-longated lung lance. By far the easiest way, to the point of cheating, is to use the longest rolling mat you can find, coupled with the type of rolling papers that are sold on a roll and which can be torn to any length. Once you have the hang of rolling with a mat (see **Gadgets**) then rolling a long one is a cinch.

If you don't have any Rips, then it is simply a case of sticking standard papers together in a straight line – you may need to reinforce them to prevent a listing or leaking Scraper.

If you don't have a mat, or if you prefer to roll au naturel, then simply roll a number of straight joints without roaches and gumstrip them together, end-to-end, in a straight line. This method requires a degree of skill, but by rolling sequentially thicker joints it is possible to make a superior **Cone-shaped Scraper** that is similar in scale and shape to a pool cue.

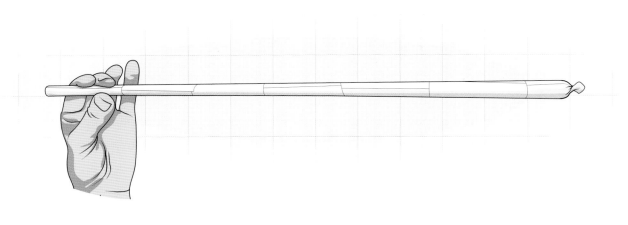

EASY TOKIN'

Anyone can smoke, (even monkeys and presidents) but chugging on a marrow-sized über spliff can present a challenge to the best of us. To avoid a nasty coughing fit, seasoned smokers never suck back more than they can cope with. Tentatively taking a little smoke into your mouth; then letting it cool for an instant; before knocking it back is a wise precaution and a good way to test the water —especially when smoking pure bud joints. Of course, another way to find your limits is to stumble over them on your way past…

64

★★★
DIFFICULTY

★★★★
HIT POWER

★★
ROLL SPEED

★★★
SMOKERABILITY

Crossroads

Three-way gourmand heaven! The 'roads might be fiddly to make, but at its heart is a roach that you can use again and again. Best of all, it'll accommodate three examples of your favourite joint in fine style.

1 Make a roach the length and diameter of a thick pencil and seal it with papers.

2 Cut two large, circular holes at either side of the roach, about 1.5" (3cm) from its end.

3 Make another roach, half the length and narrower than the first.

4 Cut the biggest possible smoke hole you can make through the centre of the smaller roach.

5 Join the two roaches by inserting the second tube through the hole you made in the first. Rotate the smaller tube until the central smoke hole is in line with the larger tube. If you can see daylight through all of the tubes then you've cracked it.

6 Carefully seal the joins with tape or gummed strips. Keep bandaging until they are all airtight.

7 To use the 'roads, simply roll three identical joints around the protruding roaches. You can attach any joint you like to create some brain-bending variations.

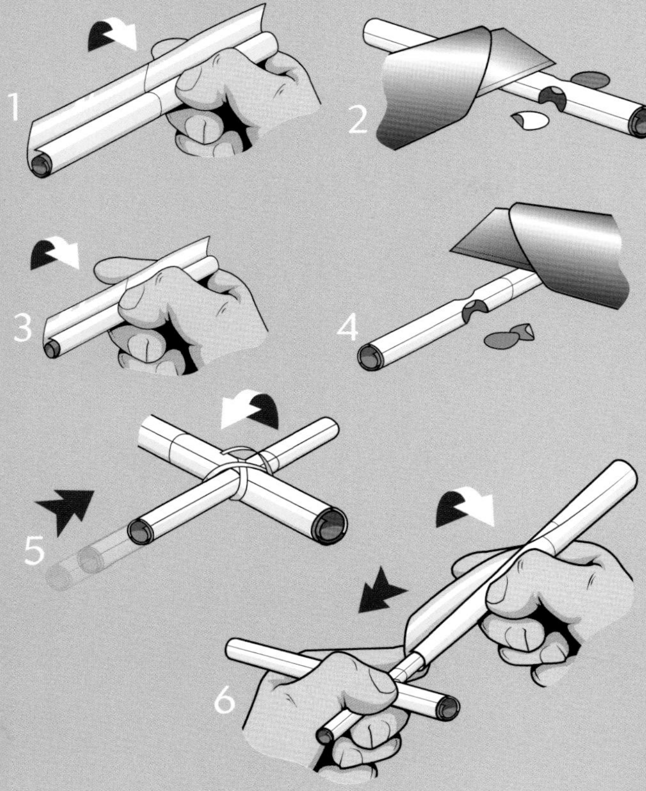

1

2

3

4

5

6

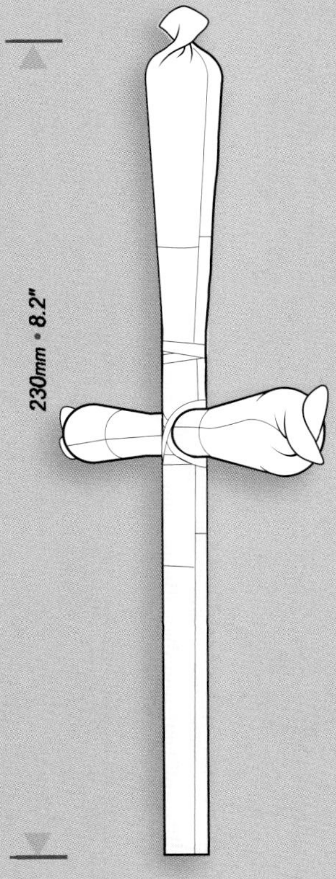

230mm • 8.2"

GRASSROADS

SHOT GUNNING

When joints get silly. Extreme multi-joints like the Ladder or the V8 (shown here) will only work properly with a shotgun hole.

Just as with the shotgun holes found in many bongs, the opening is covered during the first half of the pull and then released during the second to suck back the remaining smoke and clear the tubes for the next draw.

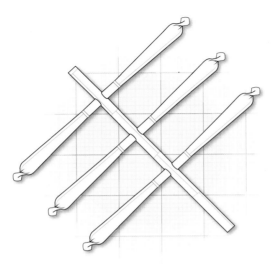

JACOBS LADDER

Why stop with just three joints? Once you have the hang of multiple roaches, you are free to roll some truly mind-bending multi-joints. The Jacobs Ladder turns an overused biblical reference into something you should probably worry about. A lot. Just watch you don't have someones eye out.

TAR BOMB

It's happened to us all. One minute you're enjoying a smooth-smoking little number and the next you're trying to banish the taste of satan's anus from your tongue. Foul-tasting tar at the roach tip seems more of a risk with tobacco joints but exactly why some joints 'tar bomb' and others don't is a mystery yet to be solved by the march of science. Snipping off the offending part of the roach should restore the joint to its smooth-smoking self in an instant.

DIFFICULTY

HIT POWER

ROLL SPEED

SMOKERBILITY

If you want to keep your rep on the block there's only one joint that's dope enough. A well-rolled Cohiba is a heady tobacco/bud combo of genuine class. Just watch it don't pop a cap in yo' ass (bitch).

1, 2 Slit your stogie open from end-to-end. A razor sharp knife is essential for natural leaf wrappers. Empty out all of the tobacco, but treat the wrapper with care.

3 If the wrapper feels dry or brittle, lightly steam it over a boiling kettle until it is pliable enough to work with.

4 A combination of bud and good heavy hashish suits a Cohiba. Pile it in but make sure the wrapper can overlap itself easily.

5 Roll-up your blunt. The technique is more of a tuck'n'wrap procedure than a conventional roll.

6 The mantra to repeat when sealing your blunt is "spit equals stick"—time to crank up those salivary glands. A sip of sugary coke should help seal a reluctant wrapper.

7 Too queasy for all that bodily fluid? Mix a weak sugar/flour and water cocktail and dab it on the join with your finger. Don't overdo it or you will harshen the smoke. Hold the join to ensure a good seal and gently flame the join with a gas lighter to 'finish' the bond.

*Despite the thriving trade in cigar wrappers targetted at cannabis smokers, options are limited when it comes to prime natural leaf. For a truly great smoke you need to buy a quality cigar. Cheap ones work fine but we say treat yourself. It's only a waste if you don't enjoy it.

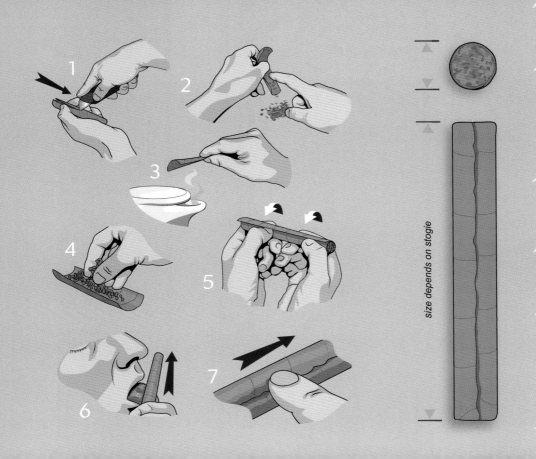

size depends on stogie

COHIBA BLUNT

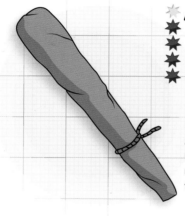

BIDI SPECIAL

All this gumstripping, joint-joining and origami-twiddling getting you down? All hail the Bidi! The Bidi is a fairly noxious (but somehow beguiling) hand-made 'mini cigar'. Consisting of a few crumbs of tobacco wrapped in a leaf and secured with a piece of thread, the humble Bidi is more popular than the cigarette in India and increasingly ubiquitous elsewhere. You can make a great little blunt with a Bidi. Simply untie the thread, replace the tobacco with the mix of your choice and rewrap the leaf. The whole process takes seconds and the smoke is good.

DIFFICULTY

HIT POWER

ROLL SPEED

SMOKERABILITY

Pipe Bomb

A pure hash joint for those who prefer their premium smoke untainted by paper or tobacco. Simplicity itself, and explosive results for those lucky rollers with access to the good stuff.

1 First find yourself a piece of top quality hashish. Not just any old choddy will do (checkout How Dope is Your Dope?).

2 You'll need to warm the hash before it is pliable enough to shape. Very soft, primo hashish shouldn't need more than a few rolls around the palm...

3 ...less squidgy offerings may need a zap in a microwave or a stint on a radiator. Be careful, anything more than a gentle heat could damage the high.

4 Place the hash on a smooth, hard surface and roll it out into a thin sheet. A warmed glass or ceramic rolling pin is perfect for the job. Aim for millimetre thickness.

5,6 Once you're done, cut out a rectangular sheet about 2.5" by 1.75" (6cm by 4cm) and roll it into a loosely spiralled tube as shown. Press-seal the join so it will hold air. A little experimentation is needed to roll and smoke a good **Pipe Bomb**, don't be put off—it's worth the effort.

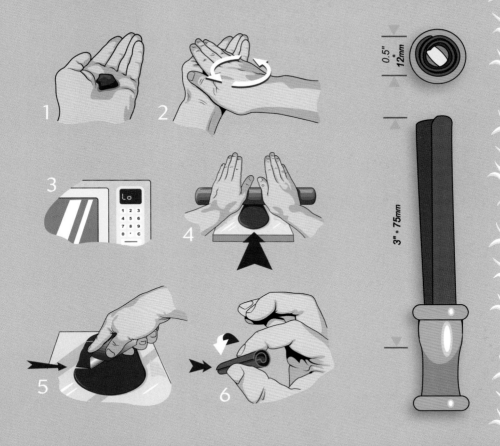

MOZZIE COIL

Another great way to smoke pure hash. For this you will need: a beer mat or some stiff card; a pint glass; a long pin, needle or nail and a nice piece of proper hashish – the standard Moroccan cak will not do at all. Warm the hashish between your palms and roll it into a long thin sausage. Coil the sausage into a spiral shape as shown. Now, push your pin through the centre of the beer mat and impale the coil on its point. Light the end of the coil until it burns like incense and place the glass to catch the smoke. When you have a pint of smoke, tilt the glass and suck out the smoke from under the rim. Replace the glass and pass the whole ensemble to your neighbour. Pub fun!

DIFFICULTY

HIT POWER

ROLL SPEED

SMOKERBILITY

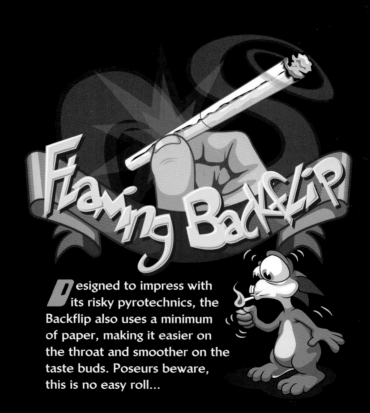

Flaming BackFlip

Designed to impress with its risky pyrotechnics, the Backflip also uses a minimum of paper, making it easier on the throat and smoother on the taste buds. Poseurs beware, this is no easy roll...

1 Stick two papers together with the gum strips forming a straight line.

2 Take a third paper and fold it in half, leaving the gummed strip on the outside. Wet the gum and sandwich the folded paper firmly between the other two skins, as shown.

3 Pull out the third paper. It will leave enough gum to stick the other two papers together.

4 If you have to use a cigarette, roast it gently over a moving flame to 'sweat out' some of the tar and nicotine.

5 Pay attention now. Add your mix to the REVERSE of the papers, keeping the gummed strip facing DOWN and AWAY from you.

6 Roll the joint in reverse and seal it leaving the excess paper on the outside. This can take some practise. Persevere.

7 Now for the finale: with the seal still wet, light the excess paper at the roach and watch it burn away leaving a perfect joint. You the man.

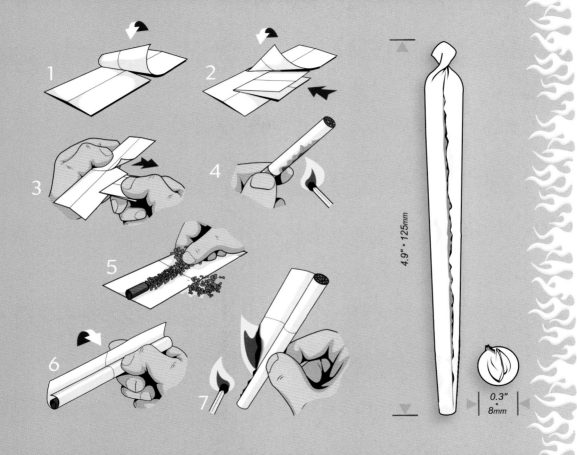

1

2

3

4

5

6

7

4.9" • 125mm

0.3"
8mm

FLAMING BACKFLIP

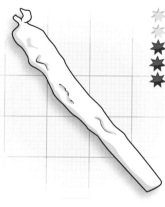

POLLEN POD

With perseverance, it is possible to roll a pure hash spliff that will smoke satisfactorily the whole way down. The secret (as ever) is in the consistency and quality of the mix. Don't attempt this with anything other than high quality hashish. The aim is to crumble the hashish into a mix that will breathe enough to allow easy toking—match head sized nuggets, surrounded by smaller crumbs work best. A tightly rolled Pollen Pod will be infuriating to smoke, whereas a baggy one will torch your shirt, so try for 'loose but secure'. Use a heavyweight paper or a blunt wrap. The results never look great, but then so what?

DIFFICULTY

HIT POWER

ROLL SPEED

SMOKERBILITY

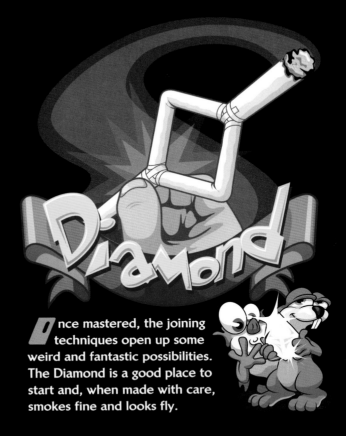

Diamond

*O*nce mastered, the joining techniques open up some weird and fantastic possibilities. The Diamond is a good place to start and, when made with care, smokes fine and looks fly.

1 Roll a straight, fat joint with a sturdy roach. Then cut it cleanly in two with a sharp blade.

2, 3 Roll two identical joints, without roaches and thinner than the first. Consistency is vital: they must burn at the same rate. Trim any excess paper from all four joints, leaving the mix flush with the ends.

4 Cut the gummed strips from ten spare papers (the wider strips from big papers are best) and put them to one side.

5 Now, the tricky bit. Join the two identical joints to the segment of the first joint containing the roach. Use some of the gummed strips to bandage the join as shown. It is best to do this on a flat surface. Keep bandaging until everything is airtight and secure.

6 Very gently, bend the two joints at their centres until they meet to form a diamond shape.

7 Finally, bandage the remaining joint to the end of the diamond, using the gummed strips as before. You are the diamond geezer!

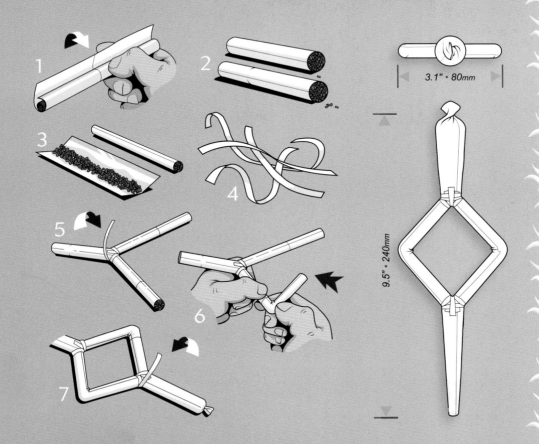

1

2

3

4

5

6

7

3.1" • 80mm

9.5" • 240mm

DIAMOND

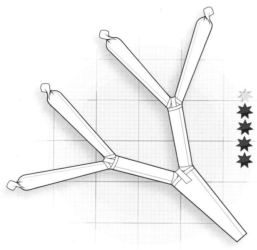

TREE OF MONG

Once you have the hang of gumstripping different joints together, the possibilities are phenomenal. Show off to friends and family by clambering up the Tree of Mong, poking your head through the leafy canopy and cackling like a psychotic squirrel…before falling out and hitting every branch on the way down. Six single king-sizers gumstripped into one fat cone maketh the arboreal destroyer. Don't do it.

DIFFICULTY

HIT POWER

ROLL SPEED

SMOKERBILITY

Nose Cone

The big, bad, bastard brother of the Tulip (try saying that after you've smoked one). A good Nose Cone is a king-size chunk of truly cosmic proportions. Earth bound lightweights should not apply.

1 Take two large papers and stick them together to form a square with a gummed strip running along one side.

2 Fold corner A over to corner B to form a triangle, leaving the gummed strip uncovered.

3 Wet the strip and fold it over to seal the triangle. You should now have a flattened paper cone.

4 Open up the cone and pack it quite firmly with different layers of carefully blended mix.

5,6 Roll a big, fat cone with an end the same diameter as your cone. A **Knee Trembler** made with kingsize papers is ideal, You will need a lot of mix, and we mean a LOT of mix. Use a big sturdy roach.

7 Trim any excess paper from the joint and cone. Then, ensuring the mix is firm and flush, join the two halves together with gum strips.

Hold hands with the Russian monkey and countdown to launch…

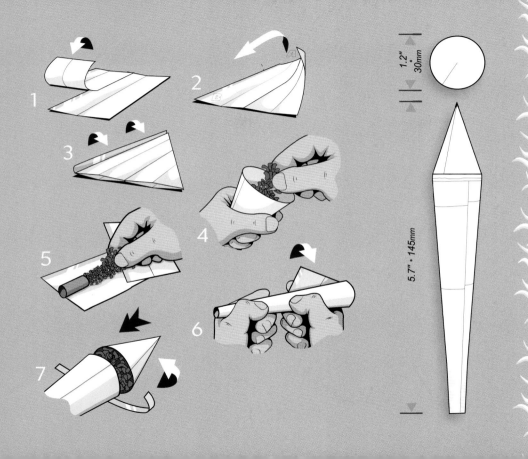

1

2

3

4

5

6

7

1.2"
30mm

5.7" • 145mm

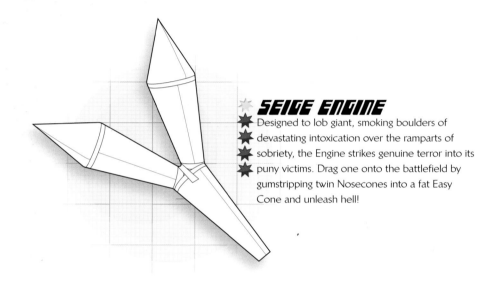

SEIGE ENGINE

Designed to lob giant, smoking boulders of devastating intoxication over the ramparts of sobriety, the Engine strikes genuine terror into its puny victims. Drag one onto the battlefield by gumstripping twin Nosecones into a fat Easy Cone and unleash hell!

★★★★★ *DIFFICULTY*

★★★★☆ *HIT POWER*

★★☆☆☆ *ROLL SPEED*

★★★★★ *SMOKERABILITY*

Twisting your head around this number might not be too easy, but stick it out and you'll be well rewarded. The Twister looks unreal, and stylishly unravels as you smoke.

1 Roll three identical straight joints without roaches. Not too tight.

2 Line up the joints and get ready to plait. If you are male and stoned, learning to plait can present a challenge. Get in touch with your feminine side and don't be ashamed to ask a girl for help.

3 Okay, it goes something like this. Bend the RIGHT joint between the left and centre joints. The right joint is now the CENTRE joint, you dig?

4 Now, bend the LEFT joint between the right and centre joints. Your first plait! (go girl).

  Continue alternating right joint, then left joint, into the middle, keeping the plait as tight and tidy as you can. Joints are surprisingly flexible, so be firm.

5 Secure the smoking end of your twister with a gum strip.

6,7,8 Wrap a roach around the OUTSIDE of the mouth end. Seal it with a paper. Finally, bandage up any remaining air holes and watch your evening unravel in chaos.

POP!

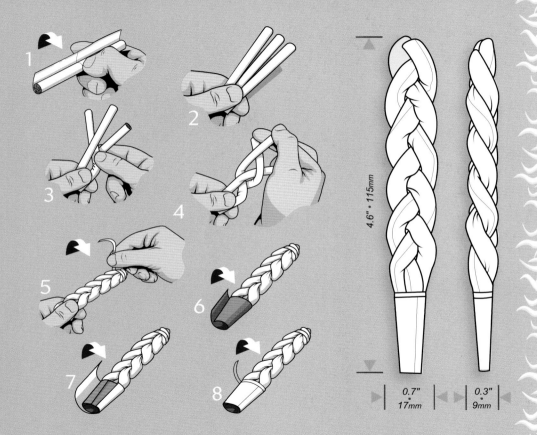

1

2

3

4

5

6

7

8

4.6" • 115mm

0.7"
17mm

0.3"
9mm

THE BLOW BACK

The sort of thing you do when you're a little bit drunk and then wake the next morning to find the inside of your lips a peeling wallpaper of singed flesh.

Blowbacks are not the safest way to smoke cannabis, but the theory at least is foolproof: place the lit end of the joint in your mouth; close your lips around it; then blow smoke through the joint, out of the roach and into your partner's mouth.

DIFFICULTY ★★★★★

HIT POWER ★★★★★

ROLL SPEED ★

SMOKERABILITY ★★

Windmill

A smoke-cooling chamber and joint holder of quixotic scale, the Windmill will get you spinning in the breeze. It's dastardly difficult to make but you can use it again.

1 Roll a wide cone from a 4"(100mm) square piece of card. Secure it with tape then trim the end to form a perfect cone.

2 Seal the cone with large papers, leaving 1.25"(30mm) of excess paper at the end, as shown.

3 Carefully make four crosscuts at regular intervals around the end of the cone.

4 Make a long, narrow roach, about the length of a pencil, and seal it with papers or tape. Cut the roach in half, then remove a section from the centre of each segment as shown.

5 Insert the two segments so that the cut-outs are completely inside the cone and facing its narrow end. Seal any gaps with tape or gummed strips.

6 Seal the end with the excess paper, using thread or tape.

7 To use the **Windmill**, simply roll four joints of your choice around the protruding roaches. Any joint will work, but they must all burn at the same rate. Enjoy a four-way smoke of quixotic proportions.

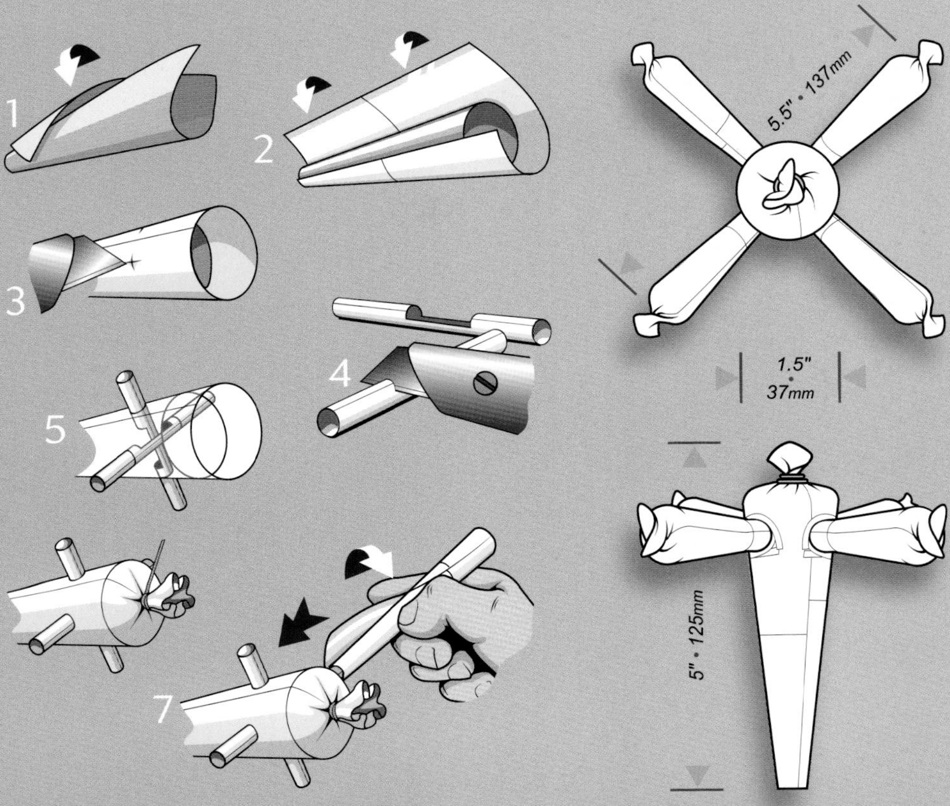

1

2

3

4

5

6

7

5.5" • 137mm

1.5"
37mm

5" • 125mm

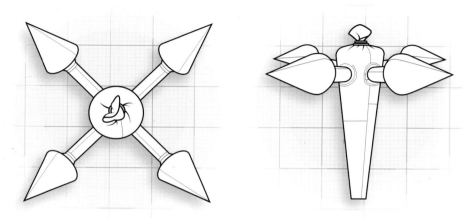

★ GRAND DUTCHY

★
★ If you want to fire a four gun salute for the enlightened drug policy
★ of the Netherlands, then you can't go more Dutch than this. Gum
★ strip four Tulips (substitute straight joints for the roach tubes) into a
★ Windmill. Warning: can present a fire hazard, skilled pilots only.

DIFFICULTY

HIT POWER

ROLL SPEED

SMOKERBILITY

A pure cannabis cigar is perhaps the ultimate joint and a must for the rich, famous and well connected. Using exotic, hard-to-find ingredients this can be a tough one to get together. Set the servants to work...

1 First, find (or make) yourself a Thai stick*, remove any thread and carefully coat the stick with liquid cannabis resin oil.

2 Wrap the coated stick with small, uncured, 'top' leaves. Remove any stems.

3 Secure the leaves with thread and coat with more of the resin oil. Leave to dry in a dark, dry and warm place for a day or so.

4 Remove the thread and repeat the process using progressively larger leaves.

5 When the cigar is suitably sized, use large 'sun' leaves to seal the cigar, add a final coat of oil and secure with thread.

6,7 Leave the finished cigar(s) to slowly dry in a dark, dry, temperate place. In two to three weeks it should be ready to smoke. When drying is complete, remove the thread and carefully pull the bamboo sliver from inside the cigar to create a smoking tube. Cannabis cigars improve with age as they slowly cure. Store them in a paper bag or wooden box at room temperature.

*a Thai stick is simply bud wound around a sliver of bamboo and left to cure.

0.6"
15mm

5.8" • 145mm

HEALTH AND SAFETY

Attempts to dress cannabis up as some kind of dangerous 'monster drug' look ridiculous in the face of extensive research showing just the opposite. In fact, with the possible exceptions of tea and coffee, cannabis is probably the safest recreational drug around. That is not to say smoking cannabis is problem free for everyone, all of the time. Here are a few tips for avoiding the pitfalls and staying healthy.

MODERATION IN ALL THINGS

To those riding their Harley Davidson Unicycles at break-neck speed along the precipice of the very edge of hell, this particular pearl of wisdom might sound like the bleat of a feeble lightweight. But machismo aside, knowing when to stop or cut down is a big part of enjoying the cannabis

experience. Logic and wisdom determine that to truly appreciate being high, you must, at least occasionally, experience what it is to be straight.

Be honest with yourself. A yes to any of the questions printed opposite is an obvious sign that you should cut down your use, take a break or stop completely. Most problems caused by cannabis have a habit of vanishing within a day or two of stopping. Most heavy users experience minor cravings in the first few smoke free days but these rapidly disappear.

Cannabis is not physiologically addictive like heroin, alcohol and tobacco. Cannabis cravings are mostly a simple desire to repeat a pleasurable experience, but like eating cake, playing video games and going shopping, getting stoned can become psychologically addictive for some people. The stage at which it becomes a problem is when there is a compulsion to use cannabis even when the effects are unpleasant or detrimental.

DO YOU HAVE A PROBLEM?

?: Is getting stoned making you anxious, confused or paranoid?

?: Is getting stoned making you retreat from human interaction or affecting your relationships?

?: Is getting stoned interfering with your work or your studies?

?: Has smoking cannabis stopped being enjoyable and become something that you just need to do?

BE KIND TO YOUR LUNGS

Smoking anything is bad for you and cannabis is no exception. It contains more tar than tobacco and hits the throat and lungs at a higher, more damaging, temperature. On a more positive note, the amounts of cannabis commonly consumed are probably not enough to cause any significant lasting damage.

More serious problems arise when smokers mix their cannabis with tobacco, a practice almost universal in Britain and Europe. Tobacco is the biggest health problem for cannabis smokers in Europe. If you're not already a cigarette smoker, caning tobacco-filled joints on a regular basis will turn you into one very quickly and whereas smoking the odd joint is unlikely to cause any serious damage, a twenty-a-day addiction to High Tar Senior Surgeons will eventually fuck you up.

North Americans rarely use tobacco in their joints, nor do Australians, and a well-rolled joint of pure bud

SAFER INHALING

◆ **Don't smoke tobacco with your cannabis**

◆ **The last quarter of a joint contains more tar than the first three quarters put together. Use a buffer and discard it.**

◆ **Don't 'deep dive'. Take short easy drags.**

◆ **If you have a respiratory problem, then you should not smoke cannabis. Try eating it or invest in a vaporiser instead.**

◆ **Yodel your joints to allow smoke to cool to safer temperatures (see page 52).**

will smoke smooth and taste good. So do we really need tobacco? Gone are the days when herbal cannabis was so expensive that it had to be eked out with tobacco. In fact, with a packet of fags in the UK nudging the £5 mark, it could soon be cheaper to eke out your tobacco with cannabis.

Another common and harmful smoking practise is 'deep diving'—where as much smoke as possible is held down for as long as possible to get that 'extra kick'. Any added effects from deep diving (such as dizziness) are down to oxygen starvation and an overactive imagination. Studies have shown that the duration of inhalation has little influence on effect. Deep diving looks stupid, damages your lungs and makes your face go purple but it doesn't do much else. Avoid.

DON'T DRIVE

Whilst cannabis does not increase risk taking behaviour like alcohol and some studies have shown that drivers on cannabis are not that much worse than straight drivers, driving a car whilst stoned is a bad idea. Any drug which alters perception of your surroundings and affects your ability to concentrate will not make you a better driver. Similarly, pilots, nuclear submarine captains and operators of large cranes should think very hard indeed before smoking on the job.

DO NOT SMOKE CANNABIS IF...

...YOU ARE PREGNANT

The dangers of smoking tobacco during pregnancy are well known and studies have shown that smoking cannabis during pregnancy may also cause a drop in birth weight.

...YOU HAVE A RESPIRATORY DISEASE

Cannabis smoke contains high levels of tar and irritates the airways.

...YOU SUFFER FROM, OR ARE PRONE TO, MENTAL ILLNESS

Claims that cannabis use can cause mental illness are controversial and hotly contested, but it is generally agreed that using some psychoactive drugs can potentially exasperate an existing problem, or 'spark off' a latent one. Whilst the soporific sedative effects of cannabidinol (a chemical in cannabis which helps create the feeling of being stoned) are showing promise as a treatment for schizophrenia, the speedy, psychedelic effects of THC (the main active ingredient in cannabis) are not conducive to mental stability.